GOLDEN EAGLE VS. GREAT HORNED OWL

BY NATHAN SOMMER

TORQUE™

Torque brims with excitement perfect for thrill-seekers of all kinds. Discover daring survival skills, explore uncharted worlds, and marvel at mighty engines and extreme sports. In *Torque* books, anything can happen. Are you ready?

This edition first published in 2021 by Bellwether Media, Inc.

Library of Congress Cataloging-in-Publication Data

Names: Sommer, Nathan, author.
Title: Golden eagle vs. Great horned owl / Nathan Sommer.
Other titles: Animal battles (Bellwether Media)
Description: Minneapolis, MN : Bellwether Media, 2021. | Series: Torque.
   Animal battles | Includes bibliographical references and index. |
   Audience: Ages 7-12. | Audience: Grades 4-6. | Summary: "Amazing
   photography accompanies engaging information about golden eagles and
   great horned owls. The combination of high-interest subject matter and
   light text is intended for students in grades 3 through 7"–Provided by publisher.
Identifiers: LCCN 2020003018 (print) | LCCN 2020003019 (ebook) | ISBN
   9781644872802 (library binding) | ISBN 9781681037431 (ebook)
Subjects: LCSH: Golden eagle–Juvenile literature. | Great horned
   owl–Juvenile literature.
Classification: LCC QL696.F32 S6635 2021 (print) | LCC QL696.F32 (ebook)
   | DDC 598.9/423–dc23
LC record available at https://lccn.loc.gov/2020003018
LC ebook record available at https://lccn.loc.gov/2020003019

Editor: Kieran Downs   Designer: Andrea Schneider

Printed in the United States of America, North Mankato, MN.

TABLE OF CONTENTS

THE COMPETITORS

Raptors are some of the most graceful hunters in the wild. Golden eagles are among the strongest raptors. Attacking from above, they threaten **prey** both big and small.

Golden eagles face stiff competition from great horned owls. The owls can scoop up prey without making a sound. These two **predators** compete to rule the sky!

GOLDEN EAGLES VS. LARGE PREY

Golden eagles are able to defeat prey larger than themselves. They are known to take down adult deer in the wild!

Golden eagles are some of the largest birds of prey. Their wingspan can be up to 7.2 feet (2.2 meters)! They have long tails, golden heads, and wide, rounded wings.

There are several **subspecies** of golden eagles. They fly across many **habitats** and make large nests on cliffs or in treetops.

GOLDEN EAGLE PROFILE

WINGSPAN
UP TO 7.2 FT (2.2 METERS)

HEIGHT
UP TO 2.8 FEET
(0.9 METERS)

WEIGHT
UP TO 13.5 POUNDS
(6.1 KILOGRAMS)

8 FEET

6 FEET

4 FEET

2 FEET

0 FEET

HABITAT

FORESTS

TUNDRA

PLAINS

DESERTS

GOLDEN EAGLE RANGE

RANGE

GREAT HORNED OWL PROFILE

0 FEET   5 FEET

WINGSPAN
UP TO 4.8 FEET (1.5 METERS)

WEIGHT
UP TO 5.5 POUNDS
(2.5 KILOGRAMS)

HEIGHT
UP TO 2.1 FEET (0.6 METERS)

HABITAT

WOODLANDS

DESERTS

TUNDRA

SWAMPS

GREAT HORNED OWL RANGE

RANGE

Great horned owls are named after the feathered **tufts** atop their heads. They have bold yellow eyes and grayish feathers with reddish brown faces. The birds are mostly **nocturnal** hunters. Their hoots fill the night sky!

Great horned owls are found in most habitats. They prefer wooded areas, but also live in swamps, deserts, and **tundra**.

EASY TO PLEASE

Great horned owls eat any small animals they can catch. They are one of the few predators in the world that eat skunks!

SECRET WEAPONS

Raptors are excellent at spotting prey. A golden eagle's vision is five times stronger than a human's vision. They can spot a rabbit from miles away!

SECRET WEAPONS

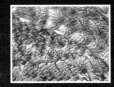

SHARP TALONS **SILENT FEATHERS** **NOCTURNAL VISION**

Special neck bones allow great horned owls to twist their heads almost completely around. Paired with great nocturnal vision, they are tough to surprise day or night.

Long, broad wings make golden eagles one of the world's fastest birds. They reach speeds of nearly 200 miles (322 kilometers) per hour while diving!

7.2 FEET (2.2 METERS) WIDE

4.8 FEET (1.5 METERS) WIDE

Great horned owls use silent flight to their **advantage**. Their wings have special feathers that allow them to silently glide through the sky. The birds easily sneak up on prey.

SECRET WEAPONS

GREAT EYESIGHT

SHARP TALONS

LARGE WINGS

PREY

Golden eagles use sharp **talons** and hooked beaks to catch prey. Both are strong enough to easily wound enemies.

Great horned owls fight with their feet. A powerful **grip** allows the birds to strike with 28 pounds (12.7 kilograms) of **force**. This takes out prey instantly.

WEIGHT LIFTERS

Great horned owls can carry prey three to four times heavier than themselves!

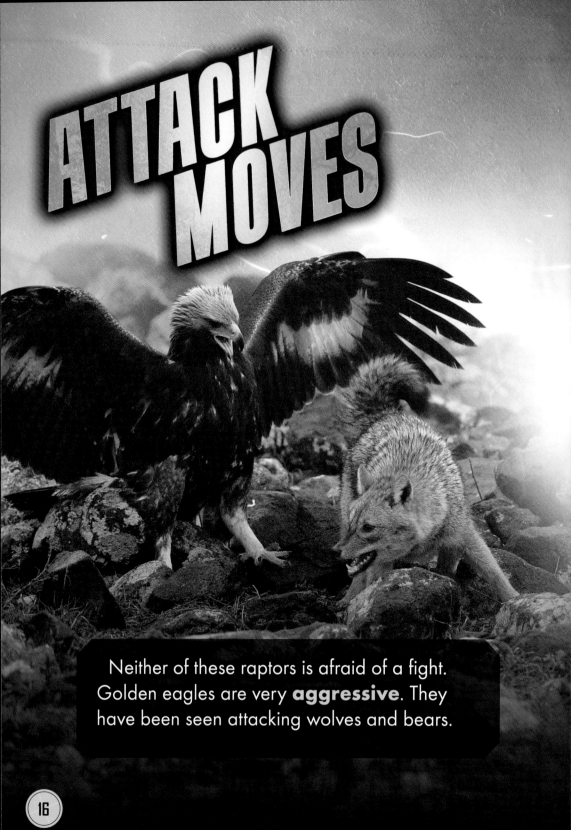

ATTACK MOVES

Neither of these raptors is afraid of a fight. Golden eagles are very **aggressive**. They have been seen attacking wolves and bears.

Great horned owls only fight when necessary. They usually strike by surprise. Their sharp talons stun enemies before they have a chance to react!

PROTECTIVE PARENTS

Great horned owls aggressively protect their young. Sometimes, they even fight humans who come too close!

WORKING TOGETHER

Golden eagle pairs guard territories of up to 60 square miles (155 square kilometers). The pairs attack other birds who enter their territory.

Golden eagles dive at enemies with super speed. The eagles often work in pairs while hunting. They fly low when **stalking** prey. They wait until the perfect moment to strike.

Great horned owls squeeze prey tightly once it is caught. Their grip can break bones in a matter of seconds!

READY, FIGHT!

A golden eagle spots **carrion** below. But a great horned owl is already eating it. The eagle is ready to battle for its food!

The eagle stuns the owl with a high-speed hit. The owl strikes back. But it is no match for its enemy's size and force. The golden eagle won its meal!

CARRION

GLOSSARY

advantage—something that an animal has or can do better than their enemy

aggressive—ready to fight

carrion—the remains of a dead animal

force—the strength of an action

grip—a tight hold

habitats—the homes or areas where animals prefer to live

nocturnal—active at night

predators—animals that hunt other animals for food

prey—animals that are hunted by other animals for food

raptors—large birds that hunt other animals; raptors are also called birds of prey.

stalking—following closely and quietly

subspecies—particular types of animals that exist within a species

talons—sharp claws on birds that allow them to grab and tear into prey

tufts—thick patches of feathers on top of a great horned owl's head

tundra—a flat, treeless area where the ground is always frozen

TO LEARN MORE

AT THE LIBRARY

Calver, Paul, and Toby Reynolds. *Birds of Prey*. Haupagge, N.Y.: Barron's Educational Series, Inc., 2017.

Hamilton, S.L. *Owls*. Minneapolis, Minn.: Abdo Publishing, 2018.

Sommer, Nathan. *Eagles*. Minneapolis, Minn.: Bellwether Media, 2019.

ON THE WEB

FACTSURFER

Factsurfer.com gives you a safe, fun way to find more information.

1. Go to www.factsurfer.com

2. Enter "golden eagle vs. great horned owl" into the search box and click 🔍.

3. Select your book cover to see a list of related content

INDEX

The images in this book are reproduced through the courtesy of: davemhuntphotography, front cover (eagle); Gary C. Tognoni, front cover (owl); WILDLIFE GmbH / Alamy Stock Photo, pp. 4, 14; kojihirano, p. 5; Stuartb, pp. 6-7; Fall-line Photography, pp. 8-9; Alberto Carrera, p. 10; Torri Lynn Weaver, p. 11; JillLang, p. 11 (sharp talons); Karyn Honor, p. 11 (silent feathers); Christian Fritschi, p. 11 (nocturnal feathers); Peter Kniez, p. 12; Rob Palmer Photography, p. 13; slowmotiongli, p. 13 (eagle inset); yongsheng chen, p. 13 (owl inset); TxakurKast, p. 14 (great eyesight); Svitlana Tkach, p. 14 (sharp talons); Murray Rudd, p. 14 (large wings); David Crane / Alamy Stock Photo, p. 15; Ondrej Prosicky, p. 16; Ron Niebrugge / Alamy Stock Photo, p. 17; Neil_Burton, p. 18; Richard Mittleman/Gon2Foto / Alamy Stock Photo, p. 19; blickwinkel / Alamy Stock Photo, pp. 20-21 (eagle); Mary Hynes| Dreamstime.com, p. 21 (owl); Jeremy Christensen, p. 21 (carrion).